SUMMARY

&ANALYSIS

OF

BEST
SELF

BE YOU, ONLY
BETTER

A GUIDE TO THE BOOK
BY MIKE BAYER

BY **ZIP**READS

NOTE: This book is a summary and analysis and is meant as a companion to, not a replacement for, the original book.

Please follow this link to purchase a copy of the original book: https://amzn.to/2OBlhhG

TABLE OF CONTENTS

SYNOPSIS

In *Best Self: Be You, Only Better*, Michael Bayer explains how he has managed to help people maximize their potential by discovering their Best Self. As a life coach, Bayer's job is to help his clients connect to their authentic self so that they can begin the process of making their lives better.

The book is divided into thirteen chapters. In the first four chapters, he elaborates on how to discover your Best Self, which is the version of you that encapsulates all your positive traits. However, there is your Anti-Self, which is the root cause of your problems because it represents all your negative character traits. Bayer believes that your life can only change if you focus on connecting to your Best Self instead of allowing your Anti-Self to control you.

As the book progresses, Bayer describes the seven SPHERES of your life that you need to work on to achieve your Best Self. These are your Social, Personal, Health, Educational, Relationships, Employment, and Spiritual life. He emphasizes the need to find your tribe—your inner circle that will empower you and holds you accountable as you strive to achieve your Best Self goals. Every chapter contains several quizzes and exercises that you can use to bring out your Best Self in every area of your life.

CHAPTER SUMMARIES & KEY TAKEAWAYS

DISCOVERING YOUR BEST SELF

Bayer opens the book by highlighting the uniqueness of every human being. In order to understand what makes you unique, you must realize the intricate interplay between your DNA and your childhood environment. Every life experience either contributes to or deducts from the most authentic version of yourself. Bayer provides a model that you can use to evaluate your life and find who you are truly created to be.

Key Takeaway: You are born unique, but life can push you toward authenticity or fakeness.

Bayer states that everyone is special in their own way because nobody knows what it's like to walk in your shoes. You were born with specific traits in your DNA—some good and some not so good. However, your upbringing also plays a huge role in your behavioral traits.

According to Bayer, your life experiences can lead you toward your authentic self, where you embrace positive attributes like altruism and generosity. However, if you experienced things like neglect and abuse, you could end up believing lies and accepting an inauthentic version of yourself. The world will also try to tell you who you are supposed to be and what decisions to make. If you act the way society wants you to, you may end up disconnecting from who you truly are.

Key Takeaway: The Best Self Model can help you clearly define your inner voice.

Bayer describes the Best Self Model as a framework that acts as your inner guide when you are seeking transformation or want to tackle the problem areas in your life. The model helps you evaluate seven SPHERES in your life. SPHERES is an acronym for Social, Personal, Health, Education, Relationships, Employment, and Spiritual life. This model enables you to assess yourself and the people around you so that you face up to the areas and individuals that may not be aligned with your authentic self.

Key Takeaway: Search your soul through journaling.

According to Bayer, journaling is a powerful way to identify those characteristics within you that you like and dislike. Most people don't want to look at their flaws, but Bayer insists that this is the only way to turn "defects" into tools that can better define your true character. He explains how he managed to break a client out of his depression by asking him to draw his two conflicting personas—his dark side and his good side. Over time, his client learned to rely on his good persona for encouragement whenever his dark side tried to step forth.

Bayer states that you should start by writing down all of your best character traits. These positive attributes are linked to your authentic self. After you do this, draw your Best Self and give it a name. You should then use this Best Self character as your personal life coach to constantly remind you of who you really are.

UNDERSTANDING YOUR ANTI-SELF

Bayer introduces the concept of the anti-self, which refers to all the negative traits that you have. Your anti-self is the character that manifests whenever you feel angry, frustrated, jealous, or sad. According to Bayer, allowing your anti-self to dominate you causes all kinds of problems in life. He describes an exercise that you can use to identify and confront these negative characteristics so that they don't control your life.

Key Takeaway: Learn how to define your Anti-Self traits.

Bayer states that it's impossible to live a life where your Best Self is always in control. However, you should try to limit the time in which your Anti-Self dominates your character. The best way to do this is by identifying those Anti-Self traits.

Start by noting down all your character flaws, such as impatient, bitter, jealous, moody, egotistical, etc. Focus on the traits that make you react in a negative way when dealing with people. Write down anything that you don't like about yourself. You shouldn't feel embarrassed by all this because nobody else will see the list. The worst thing you can do is to avoid bringing these negative aspects to light.

Key Takeaway: Flesh out your Anti-Self character.

Once you have written down your negative character traits, you should then illustrate your Anti-Self. Bayer states that you must use your imagination and also give your Anti-Self a name. This will help the image stick firmly in your mind. You will then be able to stop and evaluate, at any moment, whether it's your Anti-Self or Best Self that is in charge.

Bayer also explains that it's okay to have more than one version of your Anti-Self. For example, one of Bayer's clients has two different versions of her Anti-Self. There is Road Rage Regina who manifests whenever she feels extremely angry. Then there is Nell, an insecure girl who manifests whenever she feels unprepared to face a particular situation. The more you flesh out your character, the easier it will be to predict potential triggers and how to keep him/her at bay.

Key Takeaway: When faced with a trigger, let your Best Self handle the situation.

By clearly defining, drawing, and naming your Anti-Self versions, you are empowering and preparing yourself for any situation that may trigger their manifestation. Any time you experience a life change that brings up negative emotions, make a decision to let your Best Self handle it rather than your Anti-Self. You may not have much time to think about the decision, but over time, you will get accustomed to letting your Best Self take charge.

YOUR UNIQUE JOURNEY: THE BEST SELF TENETS OF CHANGE

Every human being is an artist because we all have unique abilities that express our authentic self. You just have to change your perspective and get in touch with your Best Self. Bayer highlights several factors that can change your mindset and recharge your authenticity battery.

Key Takeaway: To utilize the Best Self Model, you must adopt the five tenets of change.

According to Bayer, there are five tools that can help you prepare your mindset for change:

Curiosity – When you become curious about yourself and others, you become inspired to walk down new paths. By asking questions and embracing the learning process, you will understand yourself better—warts and all.

Honesty – You must be honest with yourself to fully connect with your Best Self. Don't let shame and fear hold you back from facing your inner darkness.

Openness – Your brain is designed to protect you by telling you to maintain the status quo. But to truly see the answers to all the issues in your life, you must be open-minded to new concepts and stay teachable.

Willingness – You have to be willing to do whatever it takes to become a better version of yourself. If you have to step outside your comfort zone, so be it.

Focus – Once you have committed to changing your life, you must stay on track. Everyone focuses in their own unique way, so find your ideal mode of focusing and move toward your Best Self.

Key Takeaway: Focus on the things that charge your authenticity battery.

Bayer contends that those moments that make you feel rejuvenated are the indicators of your Best Self. Any activity that makes you feel alive recharges your authenticity battery, while anything that messes up your life depletes it. You should recall those moments and activities and try to incorporate them into your daily life.

Key Takeaway: The process of change occurs in stages.

Once you commit to adopting the five tenets of change, you will go through the five stages of improvement. These are:

Pre-contemplation – You have no idea of the problems that affect your life. Therefore, you are not motivated to change your behavior.

Contemplation – You become aware of the underlying problems in your life. However, you still don't have any intention to change.

Preparation – You are now ready to change your behavior to improve your life. You also believe that you have what it takes to become a better version of yourself.

Action – You start taking the steps necessary to change your behavior and make your life better.

Maintenance – You stay on track with your new behavior.

Bayer argues that the warning signs for behavior change are usually clear to see. Most people are simply afraid of change and wait until a crisis arises before taking any meaningful steps.

IDENTIFYING YOUR OBSTACLES

As you journey toward becoming your Best Self, Bayer claims that you will encounter certain roadblocks to your success. Your goal should be to identify them, eliminate them, and keep moving forward.

Key Takeaway: Fear can block the path to your Best Self.

Many people allow fear to prevent them from achieving their goals in life. They may not even realize that it's their fears that are lying to them, telling them that they are not good enough to succeed. Bayer argues that you must be honest about what you are afraid of so that you can root it out.

You can start by asking yourself, "What are the fears that are preventing me from changing my life?" Once you have written down these fears, search for patterns within the list. Try to categorize your fears into groups or identify an overall theme. Test to see if the fear is irrational or rational. If it's irrational, ignore it. If it is rational, devise a plan for mitigating the fear. Believing in yourself and using visualization techniques can help you overcome your fears.

Key Takeaway: Your ego is your biggest enemy.

According to Bayer, your ego is the one thing that will stop you from living out your Best Self. Ego manifests in a variety of ways, some of them mild and some of them extreme. Examples of egotistical behavior include pride, defensiveness, seeking outside approval, revenge, bullying, victim mentality, and dishonesty. Bayer states that you should ask a close friend for feedback since it may be difficult to identify egotistical behavior in yourself. You can also have an honest conversation with your Best Self to see whether your behavior aligns with your true character.

Key Takeaway: Use affirmations to turn off ego-based thoughts.

Whenever you think that you are not good enough or are afraid of rejection or failure, you are tuning into ego-based thoughts. Bayer believes that such thinking is a result of fear. The good news is that you can fight fearful thoughts using affirmations. The best affirmations to use are those linked to the positive traits you already identified in your Best Self.

When you use self-affirmations, you are feeding your soul. By verbalizing your positive attributes in front of a mirror, you will turn off the noise that your ego makes. Using affirmations may initially feel uncomfortable, but it always gets easier the more you practice.

Key Takeaway: Start the day on the right foot.

Bayer states that a good morning routine is the key to unlocking your success. You should be intentional with the way you start your day so that you wake up aligned with your Best Self. Create a gratitude list every morning and focus on positive things in your own life instead of all the negative stuff that is so prevalent on social media these days.

SPHERES – YOUR SOCIAL LIFE

Bayer devotes this chapter to help you examine the strengths and weaknesses in your social life. He shows you how to engage your Best Self when alone and in the company of others. He also includes a quiz with steps you can take to eliminate any roadblocks in your social life.

Key Takeaway: Socializing provides immense benefits.

Research shows that when you spend time interacting with others, you feel happier, less depressed, and your brainpower increases. Bayer says that socializing is a form of mental exercise that provides cognitive benefits. The research also shows that there is a direct correlation between the amount of time you spend interacting with family and friends and your levels of happiness. This is a call to get off the couch and go spend time with others, whether it's in a meditation group or in a supermarket.

Key Takeaway: Objectivity is required when evaluating your social interactions.

It is usually quite difficult to gauge the way you interact with others. For this reason, Bayer provides a four-part exercise that helps you objectively assess your social interactions.

Part 1 – This involves evaluating how you communicate with others. Do you send clear messages when you talk to others? You should ensure that your message is clearly stated without allowing your ego to get in the way. There's no need to be loud.

Part 2 – How good are your listening skills? Learn to focus on what others are saying because you aren't the only one with great ideas. Practice your listening skills by repeating what the other person has just said.

Part 3 – How open are you to giving and receiving feedback? Some people have experienced negative events in their past and are unable to receive positive feedback (praise) or negative feedback (criticism). Learn to talk to others in a caring manner and also accept honest feedback in return.

Part 4 – How do you handle emotional interactions? If someone is getting emotional, don't stop them from expressing their feelings. If they are angry, don't engage in their drama.

Key Takeaway: Leverage the right tools to improve your social interactions.

Few people are born with great social skills, but Bayer believes that there are tools anyone can use to enjoy more positive socializing. These include:

- Prepare what you want to say in advance so that you have something to contribute to the conversation.

- Stay present and pay attention to the conversation and the people around you.

- Ask people questions so that you can get to know them better.

- Practice good listening skills and don't interrupt someone, even if you have something to add.

- Keep your body language open by smiling, sitting or standing straight with arms open.

- Use the right tone and volume depending on the situation.

- Maintain eye contact and avoid looking at your phone.

- Pay compliments to make people feel comfortable.

- Chat with people instead of preaching to them.

- Acknowledge any strangers you see, as they may end up being lifetime friends.

SPHERES - YOUR PERSONAL LIFE

The most important relationship that you can cultivate is the one you have with yourself. To tap into your Best Self, you must have deep compassion and respect for yourself. If you cannot even take some time to care for yourself, you will lack the energy to effectively take care of others. Bayer stresses the need to regulate your internal dialogue and locus of control.

Key Takeaway: With the right self-talk, you can positively rewire your brain.

Most people believe that once you are born with a certain mindset, you cannot change it. However, research shows that the way you speak to yourself determines how your brain is wired. In other words, your brain is malleable and you can actually reorganize its structure and the way it functions.

Bayer states that if you spend time speaking positive words about yourself, you will instruct your brain to create that reality. But if you are always speaking negative words about yourself, your brain will create the kind of negative life that you keep talking about. This is why you need to pay attention to your inner conversation.

Key Takeaway: Self-care begins with stress management.

With the fast pace of modern life, it's easy to forget to take some time off to relieve your stress. Yet this is the first aspect of self-care and self-compassion. Bayer highlights some techniques that you can use to prevent and manage your stress. They include:

- Mindful breathing

- Physical exercise

- Celebrate your life daily

- Gett enough sleep

- Take some time away from tech devices

- Engage in deep relaxation

Key Takeaway: Discovering your passion will enhance your personal life.

Your passion is anything that makes you feel alive and in tune with your highest vibrational frequency. If you already know what your passions are in life, go ahead and express them whenever you can. However, if you are clueless about your passion, Bayer suggests that you begin to try out as many new things as you can.

The main thing is to step outside your comfort zone and just do something different. For example, you can take up dance classes, volunteer at a shelter, start drawing or painting, or learn to play a musical instrument. Don't let fear stop you from finding the things that will connect you to your Best Self.

SPHERES - YOUR HEALTH

Taking care of your health is the only way to guarantee that the other SPHERES will work for you. Bayer believes that you can only achieve your goals and dreams in life, including your Best Self, by taking good care of your health. If you allow your Anti-Self to take control of your health choices, you will end up with severe health problems.

Bayer suggests that you always be on the lookout for any health red flags. Listen to what your body is telling you and feed it the right types of foods. On top of that, consider practicing intermittent fasting and get enough exercise.

Key Takeaway: Take a physical inventory of your body on a regular basis.

Most people rarely take the time to assess their physical health. Bayer recommends that you regularly perform a body scan to determine how you feel. Start by closing your eyes and then checking the condition of different parts of your body. Try to feel whether there is pain in a particular area. Pain is usually an indicator that there is something not right with your body. You should also evaluate some of your behaviors such as smoking, drinking, sleep quality, overeating, fitness levels, and physical problems like joint and muscular pain.

Key Takeaway: Your gut and your brain are wired together.

Listening to your gut feeling is more important than you think. Studies show that your gut bacteria (microbiome) can send signals to your brain and influence your thinking. Bayer argues that by feeding your microbiome the right foods, you can maintain a positive mood and stave off ailments such as depression, anxiety, inflammatory bowel disease, and Alzheimer's. In other words, by taking care of your gut health, you will be able to enjoy good mental health and become your Best Self.

Key Takeaway: Let food be the fuel you need to actualize your Best Self.

Not all foods are created equal. Some will fuel your Best Self while others will trigger your Anti Self. Your Best Self is alert, energetic, balanced, and well connected to the environment. The best foods for this include whole, nutrient-dense foods like nuts, veggies, organic meat, legumes, pasture-raised eggs, avocados, and olive oil.

On the other hand, your Anti-Self tends to be moody, tired and disconnected from life. Foods that trigger such behavior include sugary and processed foods like white bread, chips, candy, processed oils, and pasta.

Key Takeaway: Make fasting and exercise part of your lifestyle.

Instead of eating every few hours, you should let your body have a break so that it can repair damaged cells and clean out toxins. According to Bayer, eating in intervals triggers autophagy, the process through which your body kills off weak cells, recycles the waste, and generates new, healthier cells. Fasting isn't as hard as you may think. Just have your last meal at 8 p.m. and then wait to break your fast until 10 a.m. the next day.

Daily exercise is also important as long as you are engaging in a workout that is comfortable for you. You can hit the gym, perform some dynamic stretches, or engage in high-intensity interval training.

SPHERES – YOUR EDUCATION

People respond differently to education, especially within a classroom setting. When a student is failing their classes, it is easy to label them a failure in life. Bayer refutes this assumption because he used to be a terrible student. It was only until he discovered topics that he loved that he eventually enjoying the learning process. Your Best Self is always seeking knowledge. All you have to do is figure out which subjects you love and commit to learning them.

Key Takeaway: Determining your education picture is a four-step process.

The first step in forming your current education picture is identifying the things that you love to learn about. Bayer suggests that you write down three topics that are of great interest to you. Secondly, you need to ask yourself why you aren't already learning about these things. Note down whatever excuses you have, for example, your age or intelligence level.

The third step is to test the validity of your excuses. You cannot say you are too old because there are many people who have managed to learn new skills at an advanced age. You can find time to do online classes whenever you are free. Finally, once you have invalidated your reasons, you must commit to learning.

Key Takeaway: Never learn something out of a sense of duty.

Many people go to college because their parents demand it or because they believe that they need a degree to pursue a career they are passionate about. If you are learning something out of a sense of duty rather than love, you are on the wrong path. Bayer states that you should never stick with an unhappy educational path if you feel that your life has much more to offer. There's no point in wasting time studying things that are not fulfilling to you. Listen to your gut – it will always tell you if the direction you are going is not aligned with your Best Self.

Key Takeaway: Self-awareness is the greatest education you can ever have.

There is nothing more important than learning about yourself. Once you begin to increase your levels of self-awareness, you will discover all the things that bring out the best in you. At the same time, you will identify those triggers that bring out your Anti-Self. According to Bayer, you need to ask yourself the right questions to continue evolving into your Best Self.

1. How have I evolved over the last year?

2. How am I evolving today?

3. What do I want to evolve into one year from now?

Ultimately, your evolution depends on your curiosity, honesty, and willingness to act

YOUR RELATIONSHIPS

There's the myth that relationships are naturally complicated and you simply have to put up with all kinds of toxic interactions. Though relationship challenges are normal, Bayer suggests that you shouldn't believe the myths that surround imbalanced relationships. He recommends particular tools that can help you make all your relationships healthier.

Key Takeaway: Relationships must be based on shared values.

Your values are your personal standards of behavior. Any relationship where the people involved don't share the same values will always generate conflict. Bayer contends that you must match your values to your Best Self to make good decisions in life. You need to identify your core values and then rank them from most important to least important.

The goal is to gravitate toward the positive values on your list because they are aligned with your Best Self. Try to move away from the negative values that are linked to your Anti-Self. Once you have developed this kind of awareness, build relationships with people who share your values.

Key Takeaway: Family relationships are the foundation for all other relationships.

How you connect with others as an adult is based on the kind of relationships you had with your relatives during your formative years. Bayer describes the two behavioral patterns that a child can grow up with—a secure style and an insecure one.

A secure attachment style is where the parent is accessible and responsive to the needs of the child. An insecure attachment occurs when the parent is inconsistent with the way they meet the child's needs. The child grows up unsure of the relationship and thus adopts attention-seeking behavior. The good news is that there are strategies you can use to improve your adult relationships regardless of how you were raised.

Key Takeaway: Assessing your partner's values is essential for intimate relationships.

Whether it's your spouse, partner, or someone you are dating, you must know the kind of values that they hold. This is how to determine if you are ready to continue being with them or whether it's time to move on. This is a conversation that you need to have at the beginning of the relationship, so openness and communication are essential.

In case they have values that contradict your own, you may have to examine your priorities. For example, if their list of top seven values does not include honesty, yet honesty is very important to you, the relationship may not work. You have to ask yourself two fundamental questions:

- What am I willing to accept?

- What am I not willing to accept?

Let these two questions guide you when forming new relationships.

SPHERES – YOUR EMPLOYMENT

Bayer argues that your job should reflect your true self. If it doesn't, then you will never be truly happy, no matter how much money you earn. In fact, this disconnect from your authentic self is likely to make you hate your job and become a terrible employee. Ultimately, your job should help you evolve into the person that you are supposed to be.

Key Takeaway: Schools should help kids find their true self, not just a job.

The problem with formal schooling is that kids are expected to discover *"what"* they want to be rather than *"who"* they want to become. Bayer believes that all children should be taught how to discover their authentic, Best Self so that they end up choosing careers that align with their natural gifts and talents. This would help organizations avoid hiring a bunch of employees who are only interested in the paycheck rather than using their skills to do a good job.

Key Takeaway: Discover your "Why" and you will begin to love your work.

Why do you do what you do for a living? Your "Why" should be the driving force behind everything you do in life. Bayer refers to Simon Sinek's Golden Circle as a great way to find what you are uniquely good at. Work should be fun, and if you are bored, tired, and burned out, you are not living according to your Best Self.

Most people blame their jobs when they feel unfulfilled. However, the truth is that it's not the job that is to blame for the burnout. You simply haven't found a job that reflects your passions and unique art form. This misalignment is what saps your energy every day.

"I can guarantee that if you don't love your job, it is because it is not aligned with your why and hence not aligned with your artistic expression" (Bayer, Ch.9)

Key Takeaway: Don't let money make your decisions for you.

Making a lot of money seems to be the main consideration when choosing a career. People put up with jobs they hate just to have enough to pay the bills. This is usually rooted in some deep-seated beliefs that set in when you were a child. Some people grow up poor and are traumatized by money-related events. For example, you went to bed hungry, your parents always fought over money, or wore shoes with holes in them. Such events can make you prioritize money over finding a job that matches your Best Self. Bayer suggests that you take some time to think about how you can use your innate skills to earn an income. This way, you can still make money even as you live your Best Self.

SPHERES – YOUR SPIRITUAL DEVELOPMENT LIFE

Bayer describes spirituality (not religion) as the bedrock for all the other SPHERES in your life. This is because your Best Self is more of a spiritual being than a physical entity. He believes that individuals who are disconnected from their spiritual source are missing out on a great source of energy, vitality, and faith.

Key Takeaway: Anyone can connect to their spirituality by adopting the right techniques.

Bayer highlights eight strategies for cultivating your spirituality:

Be intentional – You must be intentional about your spiritual life. For example, schedule time for prayer, meditate every day, attend religious services regularly, etc.

Feed your spirit – Read the type of material that will inspire your faith, whether it's the Bible or books by spiritual gurus.

Turn down the noise – Find some quiet time away from the hustle of life to connect with God and your inner self.

Look for signs – Watch out for signs that life is trying to tell you something. It could be the words to a song, a scene in a movie, or something in nature.

Give credit – Don't assume that the good things that happen to you are just coincidence or luck. Be grateful and acknowledge your spiritual Source.

Share your experiences – Talk to other people about your spiritual life and let them inspire you with theirs.

Have fun – Even when things get tough, don't forget to find occasions to laugh.

Pay it forward – Almost every religion believes that if you are generous, life will reciprocate. Therefore, treat others with kindness and generosity.

Key Takeaway: Define your spiritual life with regular rituals.

One of the best ways to enhance your spiritual life is by creating a morning ritual that aligns with your Best Self. This can be anything that helps you connect to a higher power, for example, watching a sunrise, praying, or reading a spiritual book. This is important because there is great comfort in knowing that you don't have to carry all the burdens of this world alone.

You can also create a spiritual mission statement that reflects your faith or belief system. Bayer also suggests that you come up with a spiritual development inventory to guide you toward whatever you want to accomplish in your spiritual life. This involves rating your current spiritual life, the behaviors that are working for you and those that are not. The goal is to focus on those behaviors that are improving your spiritual life and eliminate those that aren't.

ASSEMBLING YOUR BEST TEAM

Anyone who has ever achieved anything great in life had to rely on other people to do it. No man is an island, and the depth of your closest relationships will affect your life in a profound way. Bayer takes a deep look into the role that your inner circle plays on every SPHERE of your life. He also examines the need for trust and reciprocity.

Key Takeaway: When it comes to your inner circle, choose quality over quantity.

While it is true that you can achieve much more with the cooperation of others than alone, that doesn't mean you should allow everyone into your inner circle. Bayer argues that you should distinguish between general relationships and your "team." The only people who deserve to be in your inner circle are those who accept your Best Self. They should be people who inspire you and bring positivity into your life.

If you do not enjoy walking with someone in your journey of life, don't let them into your inner circle. You can have many friends and associates, but make sure that you select those few who are committed to adding value to your life.

Your team must be ready to stand with you, especially during times of crisis in your life.

Key Takeaway: You need support in all seven SPHERES of life.

Bayer categorically states that your relationships must be built around the Social, Personal, Health, Educational, Relational, Employment, and Spiritual areas of your life. As different people come into your life, you must ask yourself where they fit into it. For example:

Social – You need people who you enjoy hanging out with, whether at the movies, networking events, over drinks, etc.

Personal – You need people who make you feel or look good, such as your barber/hairdresser, therapist, etc.

Health – This could be a massage therapist, physician, gym buddy, or personal trainer.

Educational – In this area of life, you have teachers, career mentors, your favorite motivational speakers, etc.

Relational – Here you have family members, spouse, or girlfriend/boyfriend. However, some of these people don't have to be in your inner circle if you don't trust them.

Employment – This includes your boss and work colleagues.

Spiritual – You need team members who keep you grounded spiritually.

As you examine these seven areas, rate each one to determine where you are lacking. You will discover that you need to add or remove some people in your life.

Key Takeaway: You need to give as much as you get, or even more.

It's not enough to judge your relationships by how well people support you. You must also ask yourself whether you support the goals of others around you. Bayer refers to this as "reciprocity of love." What are you bringing to their table? Do you care about your team and purpose to bring them joy? Your team will thrive if there is reciprocity of love, but if it's lacking, you'll end up receiving nothing in return.

Key Takeaway: Build your team around inspiration, exhilaration, and illumination.

Bayer believes that your team members must be the kind of people who inspire, exhilarate, and illuminate you. Your inner circle should be a source of encouragement and imaginative ideas. Your team must also add excitement and happiness into your life. Such people will make you want to do exciting things and explore the world out there. Finally, your team must have people who are willing to teach you and learn from you. You need to know that you are smarter today than you were yesterday because of someone in your team.

SEVEN STEPS FOR ACQUIRING YOUR BEST SELF GOALS

Bayer highlights seven steps that anyone can use to achieve specific goals in every area of their life. These goals must be based on the imbalances that you have identified in the seven SPHERES. The sooner you commit to these goals the better. Time is a non-renewable commodity, and therefore, you should always fill your day with activities that fulfill your life's purpose. At the end of the day, achieving your Best Self is an evolutionary journey that should never stop.

Key Takeaway: Your goals should be motivated by your Best Self, not your ego.

According to Bayer, it's useless to achieve a goal just to get it off your list. Your goals must add value to your life. This goal acquisition process involves seven steps:

Step 1 – Clearly define what you really want. Stating that you want to be happy is too vague. If you feel happy whenever you travel, set a goal to plan and save for a trip.

Step 2 – Make sure your goal can be measured. This will help you know how you are progressing toward it.

Step 3 – Set controllable goals. Do not set a goal that is beyond your ability to control. Make sure your goals are dependent on your actions rather than those of somebody else's.

Step 4 – Develop a solid strategy. Your goal may be so exciting that you forget to create a workable strategy around it. Willpower may not be enough to get you to your goal, therefore, lay out a clear strategy.

Step 5 – Define all the steps in advance. You need to know what to do at every stage of the journey toward your goal. Write them all down from the outset.

Step 6 – Set a deadline. Create pressure to achieve your goals by setting a timeline and sticking to it.

Step 7 – Get an accountability partner. Find someone in your team who you can trust to continually hold you accountable for your goal.

Key Takeaway: Spend your time doing things that matter.

You may fill your daily schedule with a ton of activities, but if those plans are not connected to your authentic self, you are wasting time. Of course, there are some mundane tasks that must be done, such as laundry and grocery shopping. However, Bayer argues that you should always check your life to see whether what you are doing is purposeful or you are simply going through the motions.

EDITORIAL REVIEW

In *Best Self*, Michael Bayer takes us on a journey into the world of a life coach/interventionist. His job is to help people regain control of their spiraling lives by rediscovering their true selves. Through his Best Self Model, he describes how anyone can improve every area of their life.

The book is divided into thirteen chapters and begins with Bayer contrasting your Best Self with your Anti-self. Your Best Self represents all the good character traits that are within you, while the Anti-Self represents all your negative character traits. He uses real-life stories about his clients to explain how the tug-of-war between the two can devastate a person's life. In other words, you don't want your Anti-Self to be in charge at all.

The rest of the book talks about the seven SPHERES of life: Social, Personal, Health, Education, Relationships, Employment, and Spiritual. If you have any imbalances in these areas, then it's likely that your Anti-Self is controlling your life in that area. The good news is that Bayer provides unique quizzes and exercises to help you engage with your Best Self and fix whatever problems you have

At first glance, *Best Self* seems to be just another self-help book written by just another life coach. But what makes Michael Bayer's book different is the way he infuses empathy and deep life lessons into every story he tells. He comes across as someone who genuinely cares about helping people change their lives. He is clearly a man of faith who is in touch with his spiritual side.

For example, he describes how he kneels and prays to God (in airport bathrooms, of all places!) whenever he flies out to see a client. But he doesn't shove a particular religious ideology down your throat. Even when he talks about Spiritual development, he states that the most important thing is to believe that there is a Higher Power who wants you to become your most authentic self.

"I am convinced that you cannot be your Best Self without having a vibrant spiritual life, whatever that might look like for you" (Bayer, Ch. 11)

Bayer keeps the tone casual, which fits well with the overall theme of the book. The book is an easy read and you can literally blaze through the material, were it not for the exercises in every chapter. He does make some reference to scientific research in parts of the book. For example, most of the content in the chapter on health was written by the medical director of his CAST Center.

This being his first book, it's safe to say that Bayer has done a pretty decent job. However, apart from the interesting stories and practical quizzes and exercises, there isn't much to get excited about. The concept of connecting to your authentic self is not new. Almost every religion advocates for its adherents to connect to God/Universe to achieve their highest self.

The biggest takeaway from the book is that we all have two sides to our character—the Best Self and the Anti-Self. The version of yourself that you feed is the one that ends up dominating you. If you take the time to do the exercises and answer the questions in every chapter, you will experience some eye-opening moments. This is clearly an author who has transformed his own life by connecting to his authentic self and wants you to do the same as well.

BACKGROUND ON AUTHOR

Michael Gardiner Bayer, or Coach Mike as he is referred to by his clients and associates, is a life coach, author, and founder of CAST Centers. This is a clinic that helps people from all walks of life live a more authentic and joyful life. He has worked with celebrities, superstar athletes, and business executives. His mission is to transform people's lives by helping them change their mindset.

Born on September 19, 1979, in California, Bayer graduated from Mater Dei High School in 1999. He then went to Metropolitan State University in Minnesota where he graduated in 2003 with a B.S degree in Alcohol and Drug Counseling. He spent the next five years as a certified interventionist.

In 2006, he founded CAST Centers, a treatment facility based in West Hollywood, California. As a life coach, Bayer helps people overcome their lack of inspiration or passion in life. He also helps clients who are struggling with alcoholism, substance abuse, and the underlying trauma. In 2017, he established the CAST Foundation, an organization that creates awareness about the need for mental health destigmatization.

He has appeared numerous times on the Doctor Phil Show and even serves on the Dr. Phil Advisory Board.

Michael Bayer lives in Los Angeles, California.

If you enjoyed this ZIP Reads publication, we encourage you to purchase a copy of <u>the original book.</u>

We'd also love an honest review on Amazon.com!

Want **FREE** book summaries delivered weekly? Sign up for our email list and get notified of all our new releases, free promos, and $0.99 deals!

No spam, just books.

Sign up at

ZIPREADS

Made in the USA
Las Vegas, NV
17 May 2024

90035614R00024